VISUALLY AND COGNITIVELY IMPAIRED

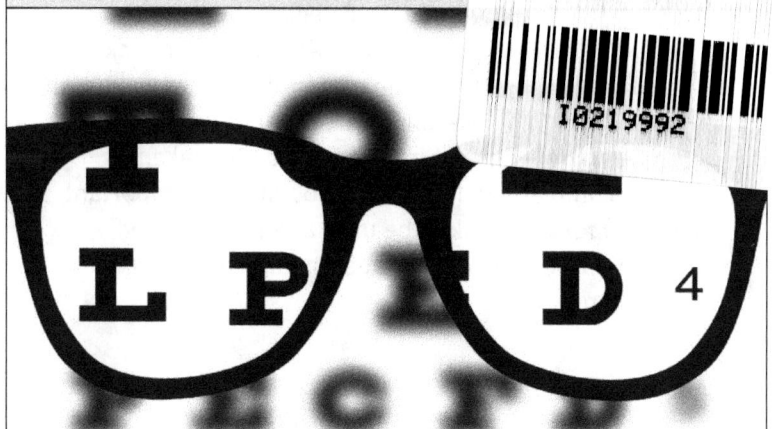

Activities for the Family Caregiver
HOW TO ENGAGE
HOW TO LIVE

Scott Silknitter, Richard Oliver, Maria Pogorelec, Sheri Shaw, Dawn Worsley

Disclaimer

This book is for informational purposes only and is not intended as medical advice, diagnosis, or treatment. Always seek advice from a qualified physician about medical concerns, and do not disregard medical advice because of something you may read within this book. This book does not replace the needs for diagnostic evaluation, ongoing physician care, and professional assessment of treatments. Every effort has been made to make this book as complete and helpful as possible. It is important, however, for this book to be used as a resource and idea-generating guide and not as an ultimate source for plan of care.

ISBN 978-1-943285-26-6

Copyright © 2016 by R.O.S. Therapy Systems, L.L.C.
All rights reserved including the right of reproduction in whole or in part.

Published by
R.O.S. Therapy Systems, L.L.C.
Greensboro, NC
888-352-9788
www.ROSTherapySystems.com

Activities for the Family Caregiver— Visually and Cognitively Impaired

This book is a general guide to Activities for the Family Caregiver of a loved one with cognitive and vision impairment. It is based on the principles and approaches used in the training and certification of Activity Professionals and with the input of industry professionals that work with those who have vision impairment. The book incorporates common sense and practical information on working with the visually and cognitively impaired and is part of the R.O.S. Engagement Program that will help you engage your loved one in meaningful activities.

With the assistance of industry-leading professionals, we have written this book for you with the hope of providing helpful "How To's" for activities for your loved one with dementia and experiencing vision impairment.

We hope you find this book useful and encourage you to have other family members and caregivers of your loved one read this in order to be consistent with approach, verbal cues, physical assistance, and modifications that produce positive results.

From our family of caregivers to yours, please remember that you are not alone and to never give up.

Scott Silknitter
President of R.O.S. Therapy Systems

Table of Contents

1. Visual and Cognitive Impairment Overview   1

2. Activities and Their Benefits   16

3. First Pillar of Activities: 23
   Know Your Loved One—
   Information Gathering and Assessment

4. Second Pillar of Activities: 32
   Communicating and Motivating for Success

5. Third Pillar of Activities: 47
   Customary Routines and Preferences

6. Fourth Pillar of Activities: 50
   Planning and Executing Activities

7. Leisure Activity   58
   Categories, Types, Topics, and Tips

8. Activities of Daily Living   76
   Tips and Suggestions

9. Home Preparation   109

10. Put Your Mask on First!   134

Personal History Form   137

About the Authors and Contributors   152

Family Members and Caregivers that have read this book:

_____

_____

_____

_____

_____

_____

_____

_____

_____

_____

_____

Chapter 1

Visual and Cognitive Impairment Overview

Visual impairment and cognitive impairment, although two distinct conditions which exist independently of one another, can often be experienced simultaneously.

In some cases, the conditions that result in severe visual impairment and blindness in infants also cause problems with cognition (conscious mental activities that include learning, understanding, problem-solving, reasoning, and remembering).

In other cases, dementias that result in cognitive impairment in adults also cause problems with vision.

Vision Impairment

Visual impairment is an umbrella term that refers to a wide range of vision problems, from low vision through total blindness, which cannot be fully corrected with glasses, contact lenses, medicine, or surgery, and which interfere with an individual's ability to successfully engage in everyday activities.

There are many diseases, disorders, and injuries that can cause visual impairment. Visual impairment rarely develops during the teenage and early adult years. It is generally either present at birth, or it develops and worsens with age.

The baby boom represents over 76 million babies who were born in the United States between 1946 and 1964. It is estimated that 15 million boomers will lose their vision or experience some type of visual impairment.

According to Prevent Blindness America, the four leading eye diseases affecting older Americans are cataracts, glaucoma, diabetic eye disease, and age-related macular degeneration.

Cataracts

A cataract is a condition in which the lens portion of the eye becomes cloudy and affects vision. The most common type of cataracts are age related and develop very slowly over many years.

Worldwide, cataracts are the leading cause of blindness. In the United States, more than 22 million people have cataracts, and more than half of 80-year-olds either have a cataract or have had cataract surgery.

Common cataract symptoms include:
- Blurry vision
- Cloudy vision
- Diminished color perception
- Double vision
- Glare
- Poor night vision
- Frequent eyewear prescription changes

Glaucoma

Glaucoma is group of diseases in which the fluid pressure inside the eye damages the eye's optic nerve and causes a gradual loss of vision.

Initially, glaucoma has no symptoms and without regular comprehensive eye exams, the disease can go undetected. Because glaucoma-induced vision loss cannot be restored, early diagnosis and treatment are extremely important to help delay progression of the disease. Over time, irreversible symptoms may include:
- Loss of peripheral vision
- Tunnel vision
- Loss of central vision
- Total loss of vision

Diabetic Eye Disease

Diabetic eye disease is a group of conditions, including cataracts and glaucoma, which have the potential to cause vision impairment in people with diabetes.

Diabetic retinopathy is one condition caused by diabetes. It damages the tiny blood vessels inside the eye's light-sensitive retina. Diabetic retinopathy affects the vision of more than half of people age 18 or older that are diagnosed with diabetes, and it often leads to diabetic macular edema, the most common cause of irreversible blindness among working-age Americans.

There are usually no symptoms during the early stages of diabetic eye disease, so people with diabetes should get at least one thorough eye exam every year. By working with a physician to control diabetes through diet, exercise, and medications, vision loss can be delayed.

Age-Related Macular Degeneration

Age-related macular degeneration is a disease that causes gradual loss of the central part of the field of vision and usually affects both eyes. A leading cause of vision impairment in Americans age 50 and older, damage to the macula affects the ability to see fine details, read, drive, watch television, recognize faces, and perform everyday tasks, such as cooking and shopping.

Age-related macular degeneration occurs less frequently in people who eat well, exercise, and avoid smoking.

Symptoms of macular degeneration include:
- Blurry central vision, even with eyewear
- Visual distortion, for example straight lines that appear wavy
- Diminished color perception

Cognitive Impairment

Cognitive impairment is a collection of symptoms that can be caused by a variety of diseases and conditions including dementia, stroke, and traumatic brain injury, as well as developmental disabilities. Although age is the greatest risk factor, cognitive impairment is not limited to a specific age group.

Cognitive impairment involves damage to nerve cells in the brain. This damage may occur in different areas of the brain causing cognitive changes which may affect people differently.

In the most simplistic explanation, cognitive impairment causes problems with memory, communication, and thinking.

Back in the day, cognitive impairment might have been associated with the word "senile." Someone experiencing memory loss while trying to locate their keys, or remember someone's name, may be said to be "having a senior moment."

Regardless of how it is described, cognitive decline is a struggle for everyone involved: your loved one, you as the caregiver, family, and friends.

Your loved one did not choose to have cognitive impairment. You did not choose to become a caregiver. But they have both happened, and you must be prepared to work with, and adapt to, the changes occurring in your loved one.

Cognitive impairment can be looked at in two ways: reversible and irreversible.

Reversible cognitive impairment can be caused by things like reaction to a medication, vitamin deficiency, depression, or an infection that can be reversed through treatment.

Irreversible cognitive impairment is characterized by a progressive pathological disease with no other identifiable cause. There is currently no cure for Alzheimer's disease, the most common cause of irreversible cognitive impairment.

Many dementias, including Alzheimer's disease, Parkinson's disease dementia, Lewy body dementia, and vascular dementia, can result in vision problems that cause an individual to misinterpret the world around them.

Although caregivers may perceive these misinterpretations that involve both vision and perception as delusional, often they are simply a processing problem between the eyes and the brain.

Common Vision and Perception Processing Problems

- Illusion—something that looks or seems different from what it is, such as this famous duck-rabbit image. Is it a duck? Is it a rabbit?

- Misperception—a false perception, such as mistaking a crack on the wall for a spider.

- Misidentification—a problem identifying things and people, such as an inability to distinguish between two daughters.

Some other common symptoms of cognitive impairment that your loved one may experience and examples are:

Memory Loss

- Forgetting where their eyeglasses are
- Forgetting appointments
- Forgetting they have retired
- Forgetting they have kids
- Forgetting they are an adult that does not live with their parents anymore

Difficulty with Communication

- Inability to find the right words to tell you things, such as having to go to the bathroom or what they would like to eat

Poor Judgment

- Making choices that put their safety at risk, such as being out in the cold without a jacket
- Inability to determine the important from the unimportant

- Misjudging the intentions of others
- Giving away large sums of money
- Neglecting personal care and safety

Difficulty Planning and Organizing

- Making dinner or lunch
    - Deciding what to eat
    - Finding ingredients in the cabinet or refrigerator
    - Making a list of ingredients needed at the grocery store

Difficulty with Orientation

- Getting lost easily
- Inability to find way back home

Coordination and Motor Function Issues

- Losing their balance
- Trouble with walking, stepping, or running (gait)
- Difficulty picking items up from floor
- Difficulty folding clothes

Personality Changes

- May withdraw from family conversations
- May become easily frustrated
- May become argumentative and defensive as a way not to let the family know how much the cognitive changes have affected their abilities
- May become more sarcastic, making everything into a joke

Inability to Reason

- Not understanding why they have to get washed up/showered
- Not understanding why they can't go outside even though it is cold and raining
- Not wanting to take their medicine because they think they have already taken it

Inappropriate Behavior

- Taking things that do not belong to them
- Inappropriate sexual comments

- Demanding and making unreasonable requests
- Not compliant with "normal" social conduct, such as talking loudly in church
- Saying things that we usually only think but would never say to someone

Paranoia, Agitation, Hallucinations

- Thinking that others are talking about them
- Not wanting to take medicine or eat, claiming someone has poisoned it
- Frustrations quickly turning to aggressive verbal or physical behavior
- Misinterpreting sounds in the house even after explanation of what it was

No matter what the cause, there are several general symptoms that your loved one may experience. As the primary caregiver, you must be as prepared and flexible as possible to handle them. On any given day, you may not know what kind of day you will have until your loved one is awake and the day has begun.

If you notice that something is different and that your loved one is starting on the path to a "bad day," look for any reason, no matter how small, that could be the trigger. You will have to become a detective to figure out the cause, and you may have to try changes to your routines because of the progression of your loved one's issues. What do we mean by this? Consider Mary and Jill.

Mary is 88 years old, has been diagnosed with dementia, and has been losing her sight because of macular degeneration. Mary lives with her daughter, Jill. Jill knows that her mother has always enjoyed an evening bath to help her unwind and relax before she settled in for the night. Jill had maintained this routine since she moved her mother in with her two years ago. However, Jill is noticing a change in her mother's behavior in the early evening hours. Mary is becoming more confused in the evening/nighttime hours. During bathing times, Mary has started yelling at Jill and tries to hit her at times. This reaction during bathing is stressful for both Mary and Jill. Jill has decided to stop the evening bathing routine and assists her mother with bathing shortly after breakfast. Mary is more relaxed during this time of the day which has also made this task less stressful for Jill.

Now that we have reviewed what some of the symptoms of your loved one's visual and cognitive impairments might be, let's talk about the "How To's," preparation, and execution of activities for your loved one.

Chapter 2

Activities and Their Benefits

In long-term care, "Activities" refers to any endeavor, other than routine Activities of Daily Living (ADLs), in which a person participates. It is intended to enhance each person's sense of well-being and to promote or enhance physical, cognitive, and emotional health. For families at home, we believe that both Activities of Daily Living and Leisure Activities should be used to enhance your loved one's sense of well-being and self-confidence. Truth be told, so does the staff at most long-term care facilities. The difference between your home and a facility is that the facility has a staff and care team dedicated to each facet of your loved one's life. You, however, are a staff of one and must figure out how to do everything on your own—unless you find help.

When your loved one's basic needs, such as eating, bathing, dressing, and safety have been addressed, your next priority is to deliver meaningful programs of interest—ones that focus on physical, social, spiritual, cognitive, and recreational activities. There are a host of benefits for you and your loved one if an activity program can be successfully planned and executed. Here are just a few:

Caregiver Benefit of Activities
Activities result in less stress for the caregiver, as well as less stress for your loved one. When your loved one is participating in activities, there will be less of a need to respond to behavioral issues. This will allow for more opportunities to engage positively with one another.

Social Benefit of Activities
Activities offer the opportunity for increased social interaction between family members, friends, caregivers, and the one being cared for. Activities create positive experiences and memories for everyone.

Behavioral Benefit of Activities

Activities can reduce challenging behaviors when the activity conducted is interesting to your loved one. Offer activities at a skill level that allow your loved one to enjoy the activity.

Self-Esteem Benefit of Activities

Activities offered at the right skill level provide your loved one with an opportunity for success. Success during activities improves how your loved one feels about themselves.

Sleep Benefit of Activities

As part of a daily routine, activities can improve sleeping at night. If a loved one is inactive all day, it is likely they will nap periodically. Napping can interrupt good sleep patterns at night.

Standard Approach Benefit of Activities

As you know, being a primary caregiver is a 24/7 job. Without help, you are always on call and run the risk of becoming physically and mentally exhausted. Please do not try to be superman and do it all on your own. Accept help when it is offered and schedule it immediately. If you do not have help from family or friends, look to your church or non-medical home care agencies that can also provide assistance.

When you do bring in help, make sure all of your loved one's caregivers (full-time, part-time, family, and friends) use the same approach for activities and interaction that you do. With a common approach, there are significantly less opportunities to disrupt routines and make unsettling changes that affect you and your loved one long after the help has left.

A common approach is key. Demand it!

A loved one who is visually impaired or blind adds another element that their caregiver should be mindful of.

Activities that your loved one with a cognitive and visual impairment once enjoyed may still be accomplished, they just may be done a little differently.

Preparation and adaptation are key elements to success.

As the primary caregiver, you are the one that has figured out what works best for your loved one and what preparations are needed to help them be successful at any activity. That preparation of everything in your loved one's life can make the difference between a good day and a bad day. From the time they wake up, to the time they go to bed, from getting dressed, or eating a meal, everything must be prepared.

Like all of us, our loved ones are individuals with their own wants, likes, needs, and preferences. As caregivers, we need to ensure that we are setting them up for success.

The Four Pillars of Activities

The R.O.S. Engagement Program focuses on the Four Pillars of Activities. These are areas that all caregivers for your loved one should be familiar with to provide continuity of care and give your loved one the greatest opportunity for success to engage and improve the quality of life for everyone.

First Pillar of Activities: Know your Loved One—Information Gathering and Assessment

Have a Personal History Form completed. Know them—who they are, who they were, and what their functional abilities are today. Make sure all caregivers know this as well.

Second Pillar of Activities: Communicating and Motivating for Success

Communication is key. Each caregiver must know how to effectively communicate with your loved one and be consistent with techniques.

Third Pillar of Activities: Customary Routines and Preferences

As best as possible, maintain a routine and daily plan based on your loved one's needs and preferences.

Fourth Pillar of Activities: Planning and Executing Activities

Based on all of the information you have gathered about your loved one, you have the opportunity to offer engaging activities that are appropriate and meet your loved one's personal preferences.

Chapter 3
First Pillar of Activities:
Know Your Loved One— Information Gathering and Assessment

Knowing your loved one's individual needs, interests, functional abilities, and capacities will assist you in knowing how to plan and engage in meaningful and quality leisure activities. This is the First Pillar of Activities and will help in designing activities that your loved one can enjoy.

As the primary caregiver, you may already know most of the answers, but this is a good and necessary exercise for you, other family members, and other caregivers to execute. The following are items about your loved one that you are most likely able to provide yourself:

Basic Information

Name, preferred name to be called, age, and date of birth

Background Information

Place of birth, cultural/ethnic background, marital status, children (how many, and their names), religion/church, military service/employment, education level, and primary language spoken

Medical and Dietary/Nutritional Information

Any formal diagnosis, allergies, food regimen/diets, and current medications

Habits

Drinking/alcohol, smoking, exercise, and other things that are a daily habit

Physical Status

Abilities/limitations, visual aids, hearing deficits, speech, communication, hand dominance, and mobility/gait

Mental Status

Alertness; cognitive abilities/limitations; orientation to family, time, place, person, routine; ability to follow directions; ability to comprehend and follow one-step versus multi-step directions; safety awareness; safety concerns; etc.

Social Status

One-on-one interaction; being visited; communication with others through written words, phone calls, or other means

Emotional Status

Level of contentment, outgoing/withdrawn, extroverted/introverted, dependent/independent, easily frustrated, easygoing

Leisure Status

Past, present, and possible future interests; solitary versus social activities; physical versus passive activities

Vision Status

Any impairments your loved one may have and what they are able to see. The ability to read standard and/or large-print material versus inability to read print. Ability to recognize familiar faces.

Informal Assessments

Informal assessments are done through interviews, observation, and information gathered through other means.

Interviews

Interviews are conducted with your loved one or with family members, friends, or significant others.

Observations

An observation is what you and others have seen or heard concerning your loved one, e.g., how they interact with others, their behavior, and their response to questions or statements made by others. This includes body language and expressions. You have probably seen these interactions a thousand times and made a mental note whenever something stuck out. Now, you must write them down for your future use and for others.

Information Gathered Through Other Means

Make a request of family members or friends to help complete the Personal History Form at the back of this book. You may also download a copy of the R.O.S. Personal History Form at www.StartSomeJoy.org.

*Note: The interview process is particularly important for a vision-impaired senior who may become socially isolated due to being unable to drive or participate in social activities they once enjoyed because they don't know how to make the adaptations/accommodations. This information should be shared with any caregiver that comes in contact with your loved one.

Assessment Tips for the Visually Impaired

- Everyone's vision impairment is very different. Assessments and activities must be based on your loved one's remaining vision strength. Some people who are legally blind function very independently. Others may have significant vision loss allowing them to only see shadows or light perception.

- As each vision impairment differs, so does each individual's reactions, feelings, abilities, and needs. The individual assessment will provide necessary information to provide meaningful activities.

- The assessment function is an ongoing function. As the visual or cognitive impairment of your loved one progresses, all caregivers must contribute to keep the information up-to-date and relevant to ensure consistency in approach or cues when engaging your loved one in an activity.

Formal Assessments

Formal assessments measure specific functional abilities, such as physical, cognitive, emotional, and social skills. They are also utilized to assess self-esteem, coping skills, stress levels, interests, and other things that could be barriers to successful participation in leisure activities.

*Note: The person that conducts these formal assessments needs to be trained in order for them to be administered, scored, and read correctly.

Functional Levels

In addition to the R.O.S. Personal History Form, you also need to look at your loved one's functional level. When planning meaningful activities based on individual interests, you need to set your loved one up for success based on what they are able to accomplish. There are several definitions of functional levels. For the purposes of this topic, we will address the following four functioning levels:

Level 1

Your loved one has good social skills. They are able to communicate. They are alert and oriented to person, place, and time, and they have a long attention span.

Level 2

Your loved one has less social skills, and their verbal skills may also be impaired. Your loved one may have some behavior symptoms. They may need something to do, and may have an increased energy level, but they have a shorter attention span.

Level 3

Your loved one has less social skills. Their verbal skills are even more impaired than they were at Level 2. They are also easily distracted. Your loved one may have some balance concerns, and they need maximum assistance with their care.

Level 4

Your loved one has a low energy level, nonverbal communication skills, and they rarely initiate contact with others, however, they may respond if given time and cues.

With the personal history and functional level information, you and every caregiver have the greatest opportunity to provide person-appropriate activities for your loved one.

***Note:** If you notice that your loved one is no longer taking part in activities they once enjoyed, this could be a sign of depression. Contact an agency in your area that provides services for the blind and visually impaired. They are likely aware of additional local recreational services and resources.

Chapter 4

Second Pillar of Activities: Communicating and Motivating for Success

Communicating and motivating for success is the Second Pillar for engaging in an activity with your loved one. The key to effective communication is the ability to listen attentively. This requires the caregiver to use communication techniques that provide an open, nonthreatening environment for your loved one. Listening behavior can either enhance and encourage communication or shut down communication altogether. You need to assess your listening style and be able to assess the listening styles of the other caregivers and family members working with your loved one.

Verbal Communication

Communication is an interactive process where information is exchanged. The ability to respond appropriately, to give feedback on something that was communicated, is just as important as good listening skills. Verbal communication is especially important when working with someone who is visually impaired.

Verbal Approaches

- Use exact, short, positive phrases. Repeat twice if necessary.

- Speak slowly.

- Allow time for your loved one to answer. Avoid finishing others' sentences.

- Give one instruction at a time. Provide only the number of steps your loved one can handle at a time.

- Use a warm, gentle tone of voice.

- There is no need to shout, unless your loved one also has a hearing impairment.
- Because your loved one may not be able to see you or that you are providing eye contact, be sure to use verbal cues to let them know that you are engaged.
- Talk to your loved one like an adult.
- Only use words that are familiar to your loved one.

Verbal Communication Tips

- Make your presence known when entering a room by saying hello.
- Identify yourself. Do not assume your loved one knows or remembers who you are.
- If there are others present, address your loved one by name so there is no confusion as to whom you are speaking.
- Indicate the end of a conversation with a loved one who is totally blind or

severely visually impaired to avoid the embarrassment of leaving your loved one speaking when no one is actually there.

- Speak directly to your visually impaired loved one.

- Always answer questions, and be specific or descriptive in your responses.

- When giving directions, make the directions as clear as possible. Use "left" and "right" according to the way your loved one is facing.

- When speaking with other caregivers or family members about your loved one while they are present, make sure the conversation is respectful of your loved one, and be sure to include your loved one in the conversation to avoid it being "about" them.

- Avoid battles or direct confrontations. For example, avoid situations wherein you are telling someone to do something.

Nonverbal Communication

Although it may seem that most communication happens verbally, research has shown that actually most communication occurs nonverbally. Nonverbal communication occurs through an individual's body language. Do not assume that nonverbal communication does not matter to someone who is visually impaired just because you "think" it does not. There are five key elements to consider:

Facial Expressions

Be aware of what your facial expressions are conveying to your loved one. Your mood will be mirrored.

Eye Contact

Make eye contact, and face the loved one to whom you are speaking. Provide your loved one the same courtesy you would a person with sight. Ensure that your loved one's attention is focused on you and what you are saying.

Gestures and Touch

Calmly use nonverbal signs, such as pointing, waving, and other universal hand gestures in combination with your words.

Tone of Voice

The inflection in your voice helps your loved one relate to the words you are saying.

Body Language

Be aware of the position of your hands and arms when talking to your loved one.

Nonverbal Communication Tips

- Always approach your loved one from the front before speaking.

- Smile and extend your hand as to shake their hand. Use touch where welcomed.

- If you need to make direct contact with your loved one, announce what is about to take place.

- Give nonverbal praises, such as smiles and head nods.

- Be an active listener. Give your loved one opportunities and time to speak. A loved one who is visually impaired can't necessarily see the look of interest on your face, so give verbal cues to let him or her know that you are actively listening.

Approaches to Successful Communication

Be Calm

Always approach your loved one in a relaxed and calm demeanor. Remember, your mood will be mirrored by your loved one. Smiles are contagious.

Be Flexible

There is no right or wrong way of completing a task. Offer praise and encouragement for the effort your loved one puts into a task. If you see your loved one becoming overwhelmed or frustrated, stop the task, and re-approach at another time.

Be Nonresistive

Don't force tasks on your loved one. Adults do not want to be told, "No!" or told what to do. The power of suggestion goes a long way.

Be Guiding, but Not Controlling

Always use a soft, gentle approach. Remember your tone of voice. Your facial expressions must match the words you are saying.

Barriers to Good Communication

Caregiver barriers and environmental barriers can negatively affect communication with your loved one.

Caregiver Barriers to Communication

Make sure that you and everyone that comes in to assist with your loved one are on the same page and use the same verbal communication approaches. Some tips to eliminate caregiver barriers include:

- Slow down when speaking too quickly. Also, speak clearly.

- Use a calm tone of voice, and be aware of your hand movements.

- Never be demanding or commanding.

- Never argue with a loved one with impaired cognition. You will never win the argument.

- Enter their world. Live their truth.

- Do not ask memory questions.

- Do not offer long explanations when answering questions.

- Do not let your anger and frustration at various situations build and turn into hurtful words.

Environmental Barriers to Communication

With so many things happening around us, we must make sure to remove or adapt to avoidable communication barriers around us. Here are some examples:

- Minimize noise from air conditioners and home appliances.

- Turn off the TV if it is on in the same room where you are trying to talk.

- Be aware of outside traffic noise.

- Check hearing aid batteries to ensure they are not whistling.

- Adjust the lighting in the room. If the lighting in a room negatively affects your loved one's limited vision, they may be more focused on trying to see rather than on communicating with you.

Validation of "Living their Truth" as a Tool to Good Communication

Your role when working with your loved one is best expressed by author Jolene Brackey, who preaches that caregivers should take every opportunity to create moments of joy.

Naomi Feil, the developer of the Validation Therapy techniques, teaches that to validate is to acknowledge the feelings of a person. To validate is to say that your loved one's feelings are true. Denying feelings invalidates your loved one. Validation uses empathy to tune into the inner reality of your disoriented loved one. Empathy, or walking in the shoes of your loved one, builds trust. Trust brings safety. Safety brings strength. Strength renews feelings of worth. Worth reduces stress. With empathy, you can pick up your loved one's clues and help put their feelings into words. This validates your loved one and restores their dignity.

Many people struggle with the use of validation. There is a concern that it might appear as if you are lying to your loved one or doing them harm by not keeping them oriented to the truth. In fact, you are not lying to your loved one. You are simply meeting your loved one where they are at this moment and accepting that this is part of their impairment.

Communication and Behavior

Behaviors are a means to communicate when words are no longer effective. Caregivers must uncover the meaning behind the behaviors and put a plan into effect to manage those needs. Your job is to uncover the meaning or causes behind the behaviors.

Repetitive Behaviors

Repetitive behavior can manifest itself as repetitive movements, sounds, and words. Typical repetitive behaviors could be repetitive questions, words, or phrases; clapping or rubbing of the hands; or pacing. These can often be accompanied by a dusting or wiping motion or rummaging through drawers and closets.

Aggressive Behaviors

Aggressive behaviors can be defined as hitting, angry outburst, using obscenities, yelling, verbalizing racial insults, making inappropriate sexual comments, and/or biting. Trying to communicate with or provide care to a person who is aggressive can be stressful and even frightening for caregivers.

When we meet the needs of our loved one, this type of behavior can be changed. We are the ones to ensure that our loved one still feels connected, useful, respected, and appreciated in all situations.

Possible Causes for Aggression

- Too much noise or overstimulation.
- Cluttered environment.
- Uncomfortable room temperatures.
- Inability to recognize surroundings.
- Basic needs not being met: hunger, thirst, needing to use the bathroom, or needing comfort.
- Pain of any type.
- Fear, anxiety, or confusion.
- Communication barriers.

- Caregiver's mood.
- Perception that they are being rushed.
- Difficulty seeing activity or materials used for an activity, which may prevent them from participating.
- Lack of independence.

Interventions to Utilize to Mitigate Aggressive Behaviors

- Identify the triggers of the aggression. Be a detective. There is never a behavior that just occurs.
- Communicate for success.
- Validate and support your loved one's feelings.
- Remain calm, and speak in a soft tone.
- Break down instructions into one-step increments.
- Reminisce with your loved one about specific details of their past.

- Find items that your loved one finds comfort in, e.g., a photograph of the family.
- Provide recreational activities that match your loved one's abilities and interests, as tolerated.
- Help your loved one to slow down and relax.
- Play or listen to music your loved one enjoys for its calming effects.
- Use spiritual support if this is important to your loved one.
- Provide consistent caregivers.
- Maintain your loved one's normal schedule as much as possible. A consistent daily routine should be the same on weekdays and weekends.
- Keep an ongoing dialogue between family members and caregivers over any noted changes in patterns or behaviors.

Chapter 5

Third Pillar of Activities: Customary Routines and Preferences

Customary routines and preferences is the Third Pillar in an activities program. Activities can occur all day, every day. The question should not be, "When should I do activities?" It is not important to focus on when to do activities. The focus should be on making each and every interaction that is a part of your loved one's daily routine memorable and enjoyable.

For the purpose of developing a daily plan of care, we will be discussing two areas: Daily Customary Routine and Activity Preferences. The goal is to gain from your loved one's perspective how important certain aspects of care/activity are of interest to them as an individual.

Daily Customary Routine

Your loved one has distinct lifestyle preferences and routines. They should be preserved to the greatest extent possible. All reasonable accommodation should be made to maintain their lifestyle preferences.

Not accommodating your loved one's lifestyle preferences and routine can contribute to a depressed mood and increased behavior symptoms. When a person feels like their control has been removed and that their preferences are not respected as an individual, it can be demoralizing.

Activity Preferences

Activities are a way for individuals to establish meaning in their lives. The need for enjoyable activities does not change based on their age or health needs. The only thing that changes is the level of assistance they may need to engage in those pursuits.

A lack of opportunity to engage in meaningful and enjoyable activities can result in boredom, depression, and behavioral disturbances.

Individuals vary in the activities they prefer, reflecting unique personalities, past interest, perceived environmental constraints, religious and cultural background, and changing physical and mental abilities. We as family caregivers have a great opportunity to empower a loved one to see that they possess many great talents and abilities. By modifying or adapting an activity to allow them to engage at an independent level, you are restoring their self-esteem and self-worth.

Chapter 6

Fourth Pillar of Activities: Planning and Executing Activities

Planning and executing activities is the Fourth Pillar in engaging a loved one in an activity. In order to do that, activities can be spontaneous, but generally must be planned and appropriate for your loved one in order to offer the greatest opportunity for success. Please note that schedules, routines, and plans should be followed. However, they may need to be adapted due to specific issues your loved one may be experiencing that day.

Your focus should be planning and executing activities that offer your loved one their maximum potential to work at their highest practical level of functioning whether physically, socially, cognitively, or creatively.

Physically

Rather than maintaining your loved one's current level of activity, encourage them to work at their highest level.

Socially

If your loved one wants to communicate with their loved ones or friends, perhaps they could utilize a computer to send an email or utilize some other technology to challenge their social abilities.

Cognitively

The more your loved one thinks independently, the more they will stay alert and oriented.

Creatively

Encourage your loved one to pick their own colors, their own techniques, and give them the tools to augment the best possible outcome.

Person Appropriate

Person appropriate refers to the idea that each person has a personal identity and history. Let's use gardening as an example of an activity. Person appropriate could mean different things to different people. Four people might all say they like gardening during their assessment, yet they might not enjoy the same activity. Each of these people have a different thought of what gardening means to them.

- Person 1 – Would only enjoy going outside, cutting the grass, trimming the hedges, and weed whacking. Anything less would not meet their preference.

- Person 2 – Enjoys getting in the flowerbeds, planting flowers and vegetables, and tending to their garden on their hands and knees each day for an hour.

- Person 3 – Enjoys indoor plants. Enjoys propagating plants and watering and caring for plants daily.

- Person 4 – Enjoys arranging flowers in vases for tables.

You can tell by this example that one specific activity does not meet the interest of every individual and, therefore, when planning activities, you need to ensure the activity is person appropriate.

The Activity Lesson Plan

In order to keep all caregivers up-to-date and informed as to your loved one's ability to participate in an activity, we suggest using an Activity Lesson Plan to document everything.

An Activity Lesson Plan is a guideline for an activity. It is an ever-changing document. It is meant to be written on to note the changes you made in the original plan so the family member or caregiver working with your loved one next can follow your modifications in the hopes of recreating a positive experience.

A blank Activity Lesson Plan template is included at the end of this chapter to give you an example of what an Activity Lesson Plan looks like.

Items in the Activity Lesson Plan

Date

Document the date the activity is used with your loved one.

Activity Name

Give the activity a name that you or your loved one prefers.

Objective of Activity

Our goal is to provide meaningful activities. People have a need to be productive, and they want to engage in something with a purpose. List the objectives of the activity.

Materials

List the suggested materials to be used with this activity.

Prerequisite Skills

List the skills your loved one needs in order to participate in this activity.

Room Lighting

List the lighting conditions that will allow your loved one to be successful in engaging with the activity.

Activity Outline

List the step-by-step instructions to complete this activity.

Evaluation

When you or a family member is conducting an activity with your loved one, documenting results and responses is critical to identifying ways to improve activity programs for your loved one. Items to document should include:

- Verbal cues, physical assistance, or modifications required for this activity.

- How your loved one responded to this activity.

- Whether your loved one enjoyed this activity. What did they like or dislike about the activity?

- Whether the activity was successful at distracting or eliminating a negative behavior. Why and how was it successful?

*Note: Make sure caregivers and family members are consistent with the type of verbal cues, physical assistance, or modifications that produce positive results.

Activity Lesson Plan Template

Date	Activity Name
Objective of Activity	
Materials	
Prerequisite Skills	
Room Lighting	
Activity Outline	
Evaluation	

Chapter 7

Leisure Activity Categories, Types, Topics, and Tips

Activity Categories

Activities are generally broken down into three different categories: Maintenance Activities, Supportive Activities, and Empowering Activities.

Maintenance Activities

Maintenance activities are traditional activities that help your loved one maintain physical, cognitive, social, spiritual, and emotional health. Examples include:
- Religious activities
- Watching TV
- Games
- Walking
- Events
- Outings

Supportive Activities

Supportive activities are for those that have a lower tolerance for traditional activities. These types of activities provide a comfortable environment while providing stimulation or solace. Examples include:

- Listening to and singing music
- Hand massages
- Relaxation activities, such as aromatherapy and meditation

Empowering Activities

Empowering activities help your loved one attain self-respect by receiving opportunities for self-expression and responsibility. Examples include:

- Cooking
- Folding laundry
- Making scrapbooks or memory boxes

Activity Types

Once you have chosen an activity from a category that will suit your loved one's need, you must choose an activity type that will interest them. There are several types of activities to choose from. Below are some examples:

Art Activities

- Coloring
- Painting
- Dancing

Craft Activities

- Jewelry making
- Knitting
- Scrapbooking
- Woodworking
- Model Building

Verbal Activities

- Conversation
- Trivia
- Reminiscing

Entertainment Activities

- Board games
- Card games
- Video games
- Crossword puzzles

Listening Activities

- Music
- Storytelling
- Books on tape
- Memory games
- Listening to the radio

Visual Activities

- Watching a movie
- Watching a performance

Writing Activities

- Writing a story or poem
- Writing a letter
- Writing a life history

Active Activities

If your loved one has been medically approved to participate in active activities and you would like to build these activities into your loved one's life, please make sure to schedule opportunities for rest after or between activities.

Active activities can be broken into four areas that all can help improve the quality of life for your loved one.

Aerobic Activities

During aerobic activities, the body's large muscles move in a rhythmic manner for a sustained period of time. Aerobic activities help to maintain or improve cardiovascular health.

Objectives of aerobic activities include improving physical fitness and having positive effects on slowness, stiffness, and mood.

Examples of aerobic activities for your loved one:

- Walking
    - with you, a family member, or your dog
    - on a treadmill
    - around the shopping mall
- Swimming or water aerobics
    - at your gym or YMCA
- Dancing
    - at home with you, a family member, or a friend
    - at a local dance hall, club, or ballet center
- Chair aerobics
    - in your living room following along with a video
    - at your gym or YMCA

Strengthening Activities

Strengthening activities improve overall muscle strength, walking speed, posture, and overall physical fitness.

The objective of improving muscle strength is to facilitate everyday activities, such as getting up from a chair, moving from room to room in the home, and making any task easier to manage.

Examples of strengthening activities for your loved one:
- Weights/resistance
    - free weight activities/exercises
    - elastic bands activities/exercises
    - body weight activities/exercises
- Yard work or gardening

Flexibility Activities

Flexibility or stretching exercises improve mobility, increase range of motion, reduce stiffness, and can help reduce the risk of injury.

Objectives of flexibility activities include improving posture and walking ability, and making everyday activities easier.

Examples of flexibility activities for your loved one:

- Gentle stretching
  - In your living room following along with a video
- Yoga, including chair yoga
- Bilateral arm training with rhythmic auditory cueing (BATRAC)
- Treadmill-supported walking
- Strengthening or resistance training

Balance Activities

Balance activities improve posture and stability.

Objectives of balance activities include helping reduce the likelihood of falling, potentially calming your loved one's fears of falling, and helping them generally in performing daily tasks.

Examples of balance activities for your loved one:

- Yoga, including chair yoga
- At-home balance exercises using
  - A Wii
  - A balance ball or balance pillow

What active activities will your loved one enjoy, and where will they be done?

*Note: Depending on the activity or exercise, you, a family member, or a trained professional should always be there to supervise and assist your loved one as needed.

Activity Topics

Once you know what category and type of activity you want to use to engage your loved one, here are some suggestions for topics the activity can be based on:

Colors

- Colors of their favorite sports team
- Colors of their wedding
- Colors of flowers or cars

Music

- Favorite music
- Music from when they were younger and dating

- Patriotic songs
- Holiday songs
- Favorite artists from the age they think they are, e.g., if they believe they are 25 years old, use popular singers or songs of that era.

Military Service

- War stories
- World events of their time—or of age they think they are
- Their personal experiences of either military service or what it was like in the States

Holidays

- Specific holidays that coincide with their culture or religion
- Favorite holidays
- Traditions

Cooking

- Home cooking
- Comfort food

- Favorite recipes from their mother or grandmother
- Favorite food associated with events, holidays, family gatherings

Sports

- Professional sports teams they like
- Their involvement in sports
- Big sporting events from their era

School Days

- Where they went to school
- Favorite school classes or teachers
- Memories of their children's school events

Old Cars

- Their family's first car
- Their first car
- Prices of cars now and then
- Dream cars

Places

- Where they were born
- Where they grew up
- Places they have been
- Vacations they took

*Note: As dementia progresses, parts of the brain die along with memories and abilities controlled by the parts of the brain. An 80-year-old may have the memories and abilities of a 7-year-old.

General Activity Tips

Environmental Preparation Tips

Provide sufficient light throughout the room, and place additional task lighting near the activity in accordance to what is most visually helpful. Table lamps offering the ability to adjust positioning are most helpful in this case. The area of activity should be lit according to your loved one's preferences. The room must also be well lit to eliminate shadows.

Empower your loved one by choosing an area of the home where they can most comfortably participate.

- If in a recliner, use an activity surface that fits comfortably in their lap, and choose an activity that does not have too many pieces that may be hard to keep track of.
- If at a table and in a wheelchair, make sure the wheelchair can fit under the table.

<u>Travel Tips for Moving from Room to Room or Place to Place</u>

When escorting your vision-impaired loved one, ask them if they need any assistance. Often they are able to follow you. If your loved one does require some "sighted guide," offer your arm, and let him/her hold on just above your elbow. You will walk a half pace ahead, and provide verbal cues of the environment. You will find this is the easiest and most comfortable way to walk together.

- Announce when you are approaching doorways, stairs, and ramps.
- Avoid puddles, snowbanks, and other natural barriers.
- Avoid cracked tile, untacked throw rugs, protruding floorboards, and power cords.
- When seating your loved one, place your loved one's hand on the back of the chair. Ask your loved one to assure you that they can feel the sitting surface with the back of their legs before sitting down. This helps to ensure your loved one is close enough to the sitting surface.

Writing and Coloring Activity Tips

- Shiny paper can increase glare, so it is best to use matte paper when writing or reading.
- Use large-print crossword, word search or word scramble puzzles, such as the R.O.S. *How Much Do You Know About* puzzle series on Amazon or from R.O.S. Therapy Systems. If you cannot find these books or others, most copiers have the ability to enlarge the size of the print.

- A dry-erase board or tablet may also be used to practice writing.

Reading Activity Tips
- Large-print books are available at most bookstores and libraries.
- Read to your loved one, or take turns reading to each other.
- Listen to audio tapes and books on CD borrowed from your local library, or from the free Talking Books program sponsored by the National Library Service.
- If your loved one prefers reading to listening, many new mobile devices, such as iPads, Kindles, and Nooks all have options to enlarge the font size and adjust the color contrast.
- Try the Book Strap from R.O.S. Therapy Systems to help keep a book and the page in place.

Craft Activity Tips
- Make sure that supplies are easily accessible.

- Place craft activity supplies in boxes clearly labeled with a broad-tipped black marker.
- Group like items for activities together.
- Store materials in different shaped/sized containers for easier recognition.
- Choose identifying and organizational systems that work best for your loved one.

<u>Television-Watching Tips</u>

People who are vision impaired or blind do watch television.

- Adjust the contrast on the TV so colors are either very bright or only black and white. Adjust in accordance to your loved one's preference.
- To make the television easier to see, simply turn the screen away from the sun or a lamp so the light source is behind the screen and no glare is shining onto the TV from a light or window.
- Try moving to a smaller TV, not a larger TV.

Activity Tips for Loved Ones with Mild to Moderate Cognitive Impairment

Your loved one's cognitive impairments may be significant enough to impact their day as well as their awareness of their surroundings. By providing activities that reinforce their past, we increase and improve their social skills which can improve their general interactions with others.

Validating Activities

Validating activities validate the memories and feelings of individuals who are much disoriented. They focus on your loved one's perception of what happened in the past.

Reminiscing Activities

Reminiscing activities are designed to help your loved one identify the important contributions he or she has made throughout their lifetime. It is an important part of human development to see oneself as a contributing member of society.

Resocializing Activities

Once your loved one can successfully participate in reminiscing and validating activities, it is time to encourage them, through resocializing activities, to build on social skills and begin to expand their connections to the community in which they live. This can be as simple as connecting with a neighbor, a friend within the church, or a friend within the community.

Chapter 8

Activities of Daily Living Tips and Suggestions

Unlike leisure activities, the activities of daily living discussed in this book are those activities that are a necessary part of everyday life. The following pages contain tips and suggestions for you to use with your loved one. These tips are particularly helpful for those functioning at a level that requires moderate to total assistance.

Energy Conservation and Rest

The body requires tremendous energy to heal itself. Energy conservation and rest can be important based on your loved one's unique situation. You, as the caregiver, have to decide that. As the day is scheduled, make sure to plan periods of rest between activities.

The simplification of daily tasks will conserve energy for your loved one. If your loved one uses less energy on one task, it can help them have more energy for other activities throughout the day. Your loved one will expend different levels of energy with different activities (bathing, dressing, toileting, etc.). Evaluate your loved one's performance of an activity and decide if it is performed as efficiently as possible. Never underestimate the energy needed for activities requiring a lot of thought (cognition)—in addition to the obvious physical effort required for an activity.

All activities of the day should be planned out to the greatest extent possible—this includes personal care routines, leisure activities, chores, and exercise. They should be spaced throughout the day, with the activities that require the most energy being accomplished at the time of day your loved one feels the best.

Do not schedule too many things to do in one day, and be prepared to cancel some plans if your loved one is not feeling well or up to it. It is better to do fewer things over a few days than try to do them all in one day and create exhaustion and possible physical discomfort for days because of poor pacing.

Discuss with your loved one, ahead of time, your level of assistance with certain activities on days with higher activities or when an additional activity is being incurred. While efficient planning is your greatest asset, the ability to adjust and accommodate other circumstances is vital. Remember to openly communicate the day's events and encourage independence in activities as safety permits.

If your loved one becomes tired during an activity, allow for pause and rest. If your loved one turns a rest period into a nap, be careful not to let the nap go too long during the day, as sleep may become elusive at night. Keeping awake and sleep patterns is important, as are activities.

Bathing

Bathing can be a relaxing, enjoyable experience—or a time of confrontation and anger. Use a calm approach when performing this activity. Maintaining your loved one's "usual" routine is very important.

Safety

- Water temperature should range from 110–115 degrees Fahrenheit maximum to prevent burning or skin injury. Use your elbow to check water temperature.
- The floor of the tub needs to be slip resistant. Use a rubber mat that does not slide, or use permanent nonslip decals.
- Place a nonskid rug on the floor outside the tub to prevent slipping.
- Install grab bars. Always make sure the grab bars are properly and securely installed into the wall studs.
- Do not use bath oils.

Bathing—Know Your Loved One

- Is your loved one accustomed to a bath or shower?

- Do they, or do they not, need assistance to get into the bath or shower?

- Who is your loved one the most comfortable with when bathing? Is it a female or a male—or a specific caregiver?

*Note: The sex and age of the caregiver can be a significant issue. For example, a 70-year-old female might be upset if a 20-year-old male family member came into the bathroom to assist with care. Your loved one's reaction to this caregiver can range from simple embarrassment to fear for their own safety.

Bathing—Communicating and Motivating

If you have to help a loved one bathe:

- Allow your loved one to do what is within their control.

- Stay friendly and respectful.

- Try to avoid arguments by offering a combination of visual cues, step-by-step setup, and short verbal cues.

- Consider playing your loved one's favorite music while bathing to promote relaxation.

Bathing—Customary Routines and Preferences

- What time of day does your loved one normally bathe?

- How often did your loved one bathe before their impairment?

- What is the process that works for you and your loved one when it is time to bathe? Make sure all caregivers know each detail of the process.

   For example, is the water turned on and running prior to your loved one entering the tub? Is a towel placed on a shower chair that your loved one may use so that the chill on his or her bottom is removed when sitting?

- Whatever the process, take it one step at a time, following your loved one's normal bathing routine. For example, your loved one may prefer that you wash their hair first and then their body. If sitting in the tub, they may like to soak for 10 minutes before washing.

- Be sure to have your loved one's favorite personal care products for familiar smell and feeling.

Bathing—Planning and Executing

- Use the process that works for the caregiver and loved one when it is time to bathe.

- When your loved one needs assistance undressing, what sequence do they follow to undress? Do they routinely remove their shirt first, followed by their pants, socks, and underwear?

- It can be awkward waiting and watching someone perform such a personal task. As the caregiver, you can provide supervision, but be involved in another activity within the space. For instance, getting towels out while your loved one is undressing is an effective use of the time. Washing your loved one's lower body while they wash their upper body can deflect this discomfort. This also creates a sense of support versus a feeling of total dependence.

- Provide privacy—close blinds, curtains, and doors. Use towels or blankets to cover private areas to maintain dignity.

- Ensure your loved one is comfortable. The tub may have a built-in seat, or you may be utilizing a bath/shower chair. Consider placing a towel on the seat because the surface of either is cold against your loved one's skin.

- Avoid drafts and overexposure. Once seated for the bath/shower, your loved one may need a towel draped over their shoulders so they feel less exposed during bathing.

- Have all care items and tools ready prior to beginning.

- Utilize a bath/shower chair if necessary.

- If possible, use a handheld hose for showering and bathing.

- To encourage independence when possible, a long-handled sponge or scrubbing brush can be used if your loved one can scrub themselves.

- Have sponges with soap inside, a soft soap applicator, or a pump bottle with bath soap instead of bar soap. Bar soap can easily slip out of your loved one's hand.

- Use a method that allows your loved one to distinguish the difference between the shampoo and conditioner bottles. For example, label one with a large piece of duct tape so they can feel the difference. Or consider buying different sized or shaped bottles for easy distinction.

- Remember to **_STOP_** and try another time if your loved one becomes angry or combative.

- Have a towel and clothing prepared for when the bath is finished.

- Use a terry cloth robe instead of a towel to dry off. Always pat the skin dry, avoid rubbing.

Remember our goal is to allow our loved one to do as much on their own as possible. This is especially true with bathing when some people may be very uncomfortable with a caregiver helping them bathe. Let's look at the example of John and his daughter, Susan.

John is 64 with diabetes. John has diabetic retinopathy, which has resulted in complete vision loss. John's daughter, Susan, assists him daily with bathing by assisting him into the shower and safely onto the shower chair. John bathes himself independently while his daughter provides support and guidance by placing necessary grooming supplies in reach, such as his soap, shampoo, and washcloth. After his daughter helps John with the water temperature setting, she stays in the bathroom, with the shower curtain closed to provide John privacy as he bathes. While maintaining his privacy, she is able to maintain John's independence and remain close to offer assistance as needed with John's direction.

Other Bathroom & Grooming Activities

Encourage your loved one to maintain personal grooming habits. Your loved one may need physical or cognitive assistance or both. It can sometimes be easier to "do things" for your loved one to save time and mess. In the long run, this serves to make your loved one more dependent.

- Allow plenty of time for routines. If having your loved one do everything independently takes more time than available, select two to four tasks that are most important. Keep in mind the big picture. If time is a factor, save time in personal care routines, and spend time on the activities that bring your loved one the most satisfaction.

- Having someone brush your loved one's teeth is not always a comfortable feeling. Always allow your loved one to do what is possible. Adaptive grips might help for holding onto the toothbrush. Electric brushes can compensate for fine motor deficits and often include a timer indicating how long to brush.

- Use soft oral sponges if your loved one suffers from mouth sores.

- Remember "gently leading" is the best approach. Provide step-by-step directions. This may not be as simple as you think. Stop and think of all of the steps necessary to brush your teeth. From walking into the bathroom, to finding the toothpaste in the drawer and removing the cap, to rinsing their mouth after they have finished brushing. Depending on your loved one's level of cognitive function, it might be easier to show them and have them follow your lead. Family members at home can brush their teeth at the same time.

- Maintaining oral hygiene is very important for those who can no longer do it themselves—or do it thoroughly. Poor hygiene can lead to additional health problems including gum disease, mouth sores, and infections.

Shaving

- Encourage a male to shave if their level of ability allows.
- Use an electric razor for safety.
- Provide assistance if necessary.
- Give positive feedback, and do not verbally correct.

Hair

- Try to maintain hairstyle and care as your loved one did.
- Explain each step simply beforehand to reduce any anxiety. Keep the task as pleasant as possible.
- When washing hair, use nonstinging shampoo. Investigate dry shampoo products.

- Use warm water for washing and rinsing. Tell your loved one before you rinse their hair. The sudden rush of water might be startling.

Nails

- Keep nails clean and trimmed. Be gentle while trimming your loved one's nails. Be mindful of how you pull and where you place their fingers and arms.

- If your loved one had a normal/weekly schedule for nail care, please try to maintain that schedule.

- Offer to polish your loved one's nails.

- When polishing, engage your loved one in conversation.

- Avoid trimming toenails—utilize a podiatrist when possible.

Grooming and how we feel about how we look can play a significant role in our outlook for the day. For some, they say they really do not care how they look, but for most of us, we took pride in our appearance. Just because we have a visual impairment or even mild dementia, this does not change. Consider Donna and Liz.

Donna is a 71-year-old retired teacher. Donna took great pride in her appearance throughout her lifetime. Donna's vision loss has affected her ability to style her hair, pick out clothing, and apply her own makeup. Donna's daughter, Liz, realizes that her mother always feels better about herself when she looks nice. Liz appreciates her mother's pride in her appearance and assists Donna daily with her hairstyle, makeup application, and clothing choices. Liz also makes an effort to schedule regular salon appointments at the beauty parlor Donna has gone to for years. The daily grooming routine and scheduled outings have not only maintained Donna's grooming preferences and her self-respect; but also provide opportunities for social interaction, mother-daughter bonding, and enjoyable experiences shared between Donna and Liz.

Toileting or Using the Bathroom

- Learn your loved one's individual habits and routines for using the toilet. Acknowledge that declining cognitive function or other factors might influence and change your loved one's toileting habits.

- Encourage toileting on rising, before and after meals, and at bedtime at minimum.

- If your loved one is having difficulty with communication, please observe for signs of agitation—pulling at their clothes or walking/pacing restlessly. This may indicate they need to use the bathroom.

- Assist with clothing as needed. Be positive and pleasant while assisting.

- Provide verbal cues and instructions as needed. Be "gently guiding," not controlling or demanding.

Clothing

Clothing—Know Your Loved One

- Initially, clothing choices should remain as they had been and based on your loved one's available wardrobe.

- If personal care is a challenge, clothes need to be comfortable and easy to remove, especially to go to bathroom.

- Choose clothes that are loose fitting and have elastic waistbands.

- If possible, choose clothing that opens in the front, not the back. This prevents your loved one from having to reach behind the body and allows the feeling of independence from dressing one's self.

- For those individuals with motor deficits, when purchasing new clothes, look for clothing with large, flat buttons; Velcro closures; or zippers.

- To assist your loved one with zipping pants or a jacket, attach a zipper pull or leather loop on the end of the zipper.

- If bending and tying shoes is problematic, consider slip-on shoes.

Clothing—Routines and Preferences

- If your loved one has trouble paying attention and making choices, you may have to limit the choice of clothing, and leave only two outfit options in the room at a time.

- If your loved one wants to wear the same thing every day, and if you can afford it, buy three or four sets of the same clothing.

Clothing—Planning and Executing

- Clothes should be laid out according to what goes on first.

- Avoid clothes that are most difficult for your loved one—such as panty hose, knee-high nylons, tight socks, or high heels.

- Avoid flip-flop type sandals or backless slippers, as they can be a safety hazard.

- Make sure that items are not inside out and that buttons, zips, and fasteners are all undone before handing the clothes to your loved one.

Dressing and Undressing

Dressing—Know Your Loved One

Your loved one may just need verbal cues and instructions on dressing. Please remember to allow independent dressing as much as possible to foster an ongoing sense of dignity and independence. As the primary caregiver, you will have to be the judge as to when all caregivers need to begin assisting your loved one with dressing.

Dressing—Communicating and Motivating

- Use short, simple sentences, and provide instruction as needed.
- If your loved one experiences an inability to sustain attention, give instructions in very short steps, such as, "Now put

your arm through the sleeve." It may help to use actions to demonstrate these instructions.

- Remember to inquire about going to the toilet before getting dressed.
- Avoid "hovering" while your loved one is dressing. You need to be available as needed during the process, but you can do something like make the bed or straighten up so your loved one does not feel slow, incompetent, or that you are waiting on them.

Dressing—Routines and Preferences

If you must help your loved one to get dressed, here are some tips:

- Does your loved one get dressed first thing in the morning—before breakfast or after breakfast?
- Does your loved one change into pajamas right before bed—or after dinner?
- Try to maintain your loved one's preferred routine for as long as possible.

- Little things matter. For example, your loved one may like to put on all underwear before putting on anything else.

Dressing—Planning and Executing

- Think about privacy. Make sure that blinds or curtains are closed and that no one will walk in and disturb your loved one while dressing.
- If mistakes are made—for example, by putting something on the wrong way—be tactful, or find a way for both of you to laugh about it.

Meals

General Information

- Limit distractions. Serve meals in quiet surroundings, away from the television and other activities. Be sure to have your loved one sit with the sunlight behind them to avoid glare.
- Your loved one might not be able to tell if something is too hot to eat

or drink. Always test the temperature of foods and beverages before serving.

- Allow your loved one plenty of time to eat. It may take an hour or longer to finish a snack or meal.
- Make meals an enjoyable social event so everyone looks forward to the experience.
- Evaluate your loved one's level of independence, and encourage them to participate at levels that provide success.

Meals—Know Your Loved One

- Can your loved one feed themselves?
- Keep long-standing personal preferences in mind when preparing food. **_However_**, be aware that your loved one may suddenly develop new food preferences or reject foods that were liked in the past.

Meals—Communicating and Motivating

- Use short, simple sentences.

- Provide verbal cues/instructions as needed. Remember to be "gently guiding."

- Avoid phrases such as "here" or "there" when communicating with your visually impaired loved one. For example, saying, "Here is your coffee Mom," is not accurate or specific and can be confusing for your loved one. "Mom, your plate is directly in front of you, and I placed your coffee above it on your right" is more specific.

- Give your loved one your full attention. Provide direct eye contact.

- Always smile, talk calmly and gently.

- Do not argue, or try to explain "why."

<u>Meals—Routines and Preferences</u>

- No matter what time of day breakfast, lunch, and dinner are served, be consistent every day.

- Offer snacks throughout the day.

- Does your loved one eat their meals at the kitchen table, bedside, or dining room table?
- Factor the length of time it takes your loved one to finish snacks and meals into the overall schedule of the day.

Meals—Planning and Executing

Eating a meal can be a challenge for your visually impaired loved one with declining cognitive function. There are several areas that need to be considered, e.g., physical ailments and changes in food preferences and dietary restrictions. Here are some simple techniques that can help reduce mealtime problems:

Meal Preparation for a Loved One with Mild Cognitive Deficit Symptoms

- If your loved one wants to assist in making a meal:
    - Make sure cabinets are organized with each item labeled with large easy-to-read labels.

- Use simple step-by-step instructions.
- You or another caregiver should perform tasks utilizing knives or operating the stove and/or oven.
- When using a stove top, use the back burners, and turn the pot handles inward toward the back of the stove to avoid any potential grabbing of the pots or pans.

• If for some reason you are not there to supervise:

- Avoid meals that require the use of the stove. Your loved one may not remember to turn off the stove. They may not be able to distinguish between a pot that is hot or cold.
- Lay out the ingredients of a meal on the counter or in the refrigerator in labeled containers. Place them in the order that your loved one will use them (similar to laying out their clothes at night).

- Transfer bulk items, including milk, from a larger container to a smaller container that is easier to lift and pour.

Appropriate Lighting

- Reduce glare by having your loved one sit with the sunlight behind them when eating.
- Use lighting that illuminates the entire dining space and makes objects as visible as possible, as well as reducing shadows or reflections.
- Adjust lighting above the table to help enhance as much detail as possible.

Setting the Table and Serving

- Set each place setting the same way for every meal. Set it the way your loved one is used to, for example:
    - Knife and spoon to the right of the plate.
    - Fork and napkin to the left of the plate.

- ○ Glass or cup above the plate to the right or left, depending on whether your loved one is left- or right-handed.

- Decide how to set the rest of the table—main dish, side dishes, seasonings, and condiments. Do it the same way each day. Learn if you will be serving food "family style" or "buffet style." Know your loved one's routines and preferences.

- Provide your loved one the opportunity to assist in setting the table.

- When pouring a light-colored drink, such as milk, use a dark glass.

- When pouring a dark-colored drink, such as cola, use a white glass.

- Avoid clear glasses. They can disappear from view.

- Use white dishes when eating dark-colored food, and use dark dishes when eating light-colored food.

- To make dishes easier to find on the table, use a tablecloth or placemats that are the opposite color of the dishes.

- Fiesta ware brand dishes have colors (yellow/tangerine) that contrast with most foods so they can be easily seen and will enhance visual perception.

- There should be a clear visual distinction between the table, the dishes, and the food.

- Use solid colors with no distracting patterns.

- The use of plate guards, dishes with built-in rims, and nonslip or suction bases can help to avoid common feeding frustrations, thus making eating more enjoyable.

- When serving food, describe the position of food on the plate by using a clock simulation. The meat is located at 3 o'clock, the potatoes are at 6 o'clock, etc. If more help is needed, the person will ask.

Remember as we prepare for our loved one to eat, our goal is to set them up for success and minimize failure. This includes removing distractions that might seem overwhelming. Consider Rose and Steve.

Rose is an 89-year-old with cataracts who was recently diagnosed with dementia after her husband, Steve, noticed memory problems and aggressive tendencies. It also appeared, to her husband, that Rose was experiencing hallucinations when she began talking to people that were not in the room or in reply to the voices on the television.

Rose and her husband have always enjoyed their mealtimes together during their 55 years of marriage. To maintain mealtime socialization and decrease frustrations during meals, Steve turns off the television and assists Rose to the dining room table where distractions are limited. Because of Rose's visual and cognitive impairments, she has difficulty seeing and remembering how to use dinnerware utensils, so Steve cuts up her food, butters bread, assists with the pouring of condiments, and provides her with verbal cues while she feeds herself. John has found that these approaches have helped Rose to maintain the highest levels of independence possible. This, in turn, has resulted in less frustration and aggressiveness during mealtimes.

Eating

This simple, everyday activity requires more maneuvering of objects for someone who is visually impaired. Your loved one may need to develop techniques for items a sighted person may take for granted. Examples include:

"Center Out to Edges" Technique

- Buttering Bread
    - If your loved one can't see how much butter is on a butter dish, help them explore by sliding the knife lightly across the top of the butter to get an idea of where to cut into it.

- Help your loved one put the piece of butter in the center of the bread, and spread the butter out to the edges of the bread.
- The same "center out to edges" technique works equally well for anything of spreadable consistency, making it easier to prepare a sandwich or even ice a cake.

Seasoning Food

- Salt and Pepper
    - Instead of shaking salt and pepper directly onto the food, suggest that your loved one shake it into the palm of their hand.
    - Have your loved one pinch and sprinkle the salt and pepper over the food and then taste it.
    - Have your loved one add more salt and pepper in small increments until they have just the right amount.

- Condiments
    - The previous techniques can be adapted to condiments like ketchup and mustard by placing them to one side of your loved one's plate rather than directly on the food.
- Liquid Seasonings
    - The previous techniques can be adapted to liquid seasonings, such as soy sauce or salad dressing—put them in a separate dish and add to the food using a spoon.

<u>Cutting Meat</u>

- Have your loved one locate one edge of the meat with the knife and keep the knife there.
- Have your loved one place the fork into the steak about a half-inch from the edge.
- Starting at the edge, have your loved one cut a small semicircle around the fork.

- Encourage your loved one to keep the knife at the edge of the meat while they eat each cut piece.

- Help your loved one repeat the process, and with very little practice it will become automatic.

It is completely appropriate to ask if your loved one would like any assistance.

Chapter 9

Home Preparation

You and your loved one need to feel comfortable, capable, and safe in your home. As the Four Pillars of Engagement are the foundation for all activities, preparation of your home is crucial.

General Organization and Environment

When organizing your loved one's environment, be sure to do it **_with_** them, not for them. It is likely they may already have some sort of system in place.

The following are general tips that caregivers and family members can use to prepare the home to accommodate your loved one's needs. Decide what works for you and your loved one.

- Assign everything to a place in the home.

- Always put each item back in its place when finished with the item.

- Organize like objects in the same area whenever possible, e.g., incoming mail, emergency phone numbers, and shopping lists.

- Label drawers and cabinets.

- Leave doors fully opened or closed. A door ajar can be confusing, especially for a person with partial sight, when moving from one room to another.

- Make sure there is easy access to a telephone.

Home Safety Checklist: Bedroom

Issue	Y/N	Options
Lighting Is lighting adequate?		Add light-sensored night-light. Place touch lamp on nightstand. Place rope lighting along hallway leading to bathroom.
Room Clutter Is there too much furniture, too many extra pillows, or too many "stacks of stuff"?		Remove ALL extra furnishings and unnecessary "stacks of stuff." Leave favorite items.
Furniture Clutter Are dresser and nightstand cluttered?		Remove ALL items from nightstand that are not functional and needed. Leave the following items: lamp, phone, plastic drinking glass with top and straw, place for reading glasses and hearing aids. Remove ALL unnecessary items from top of dresser to avoid confusion. Remove unnecessary items and box for storage, donation, or disposal.

Home Safety Checklist: Bedroom		
Issue	Y/N	Options
Tripping Hazards		
Are there tripping hazards?		Remove all throw and scatter rugs. Fix or replace loose floorboards.
Are there rugs or carpets that can be tripped on?		Have professionals restretch loose carpeting to remove lumps and ridges if needed.
Are cords from lamps, TV, or radio out of the way?		Move cords out of walking area. Bundle cords together and attach to baseboards or behind furniture.
Are pathways clear?		Remove any loose items from floor or pathway from room. Organize and box for proper storage, donation, or disposal.
Is there enough room for walking aids?		Make pathway wide enough to accommodate people, wheelchairs, and walking aids.
Furniture		
Is furniture sturdy enough to provide support if needed?		Antique bedside tables should be replaced with sturdy nightstands.
		If possible, there should be a chair with sturdy arms and legs that is the same height as the bed.
Is bed a sensible height to get into and out of?		Sensible height is if person's thighs are parallel to the floor and feet are flat on the floor when seated on edge of the bed.
		Change out decorative bed frame for a practical bed frame if necessary.

Home Safety Checklist: Bedroom		
Issue	Y/N	Options
Bedding Is it sensible and practical? Is it too heavy to be moved easily? Is there an electric blanket or heating pad?		Without removing your loved one's favorite blanket, lighten covers as much as possible. Never use electric blankets or electric mattress pads. Only use heating pads in chairs and never use for extended sleeping hours.

Home Safety Checklist: Closets

Issue	Y/N	Options
Lighting		
Is lighting adequate?		Install task lighting if needed.
Is light pull chain easily accessible?		If possible, change pull chain light fixture to light fixture with switch.
Shelving		
Are shelves easy to reach?		Shelving should be located at a height that person using it can reach items without stretching.
Are shelves original from builder?		Consider removing original shelving from builder and replacing with new, easier-access shelves.
Shoes		
Can shoes be reached without bending over?		If bending is an issue, consider installing an over-the-door shoe rack.
Clothing		
Is closet full of clothing that is no longer being worn?		Never remove your loved one's favorite outfit. Remove unworn or worn out clothing. Leave choices that are easy to match. Keep clothes that are easy to put on and take off.
Are shelves stuffed with a hodgepodge of items that may tumble and fall?		Resolve shelving issue by removing unneeded items and organizing items to box and store, donate, or dispose of.

Home Safety Checklist: Bathroom

Issue	Y/N	Options
Lighting Is lighting adequate? Is light switch easily accessible?		Install task lighting if needed. Change pull chain light to light with switch if possible.
Color Contrast Is the bathroom all white or light colors?		Change wall color so it contrasts with fixtures and counters.
Toilet Is toilet at a height that allows your loved one to sit and stand comfortably?		If possible, add a seat riser or a 3-in-1 commode over the toilet. If possible, replace toilet with a taller model. If possible, install grab bars on both sides at an angle that best suits person who needs them the most.
Mirror Is mirror positioned for sitting and standing? Does mirror cause fear or confusion?		Mirrors may need to be covered or removed for those with dementia as the person may no longer recognize themselves. Mirrors can be removed or covered with a window shade that can be raised or lowered.
Floor Mats and Rugs Is the bathroom floor all white or light colors?		Use rug that is secured with double-sided tape or non-skid padding. Don't use a dark rug—a person with dementia may mistake a dark rug for a hole in the floor.

Home Safety Checklist: Bathroom

Issue	Y/N	Options
Additional Seating Is the bathroom large enough for a chair?		Use a chair in the bathroom to help your loved one while drying themselves after bath or to rest as needed.
Temperature Is the bathroom warm enough?		Some people may get cold easily and need the bathroom warmer than others. A portable heater could be used to warm the bathroom prior to use, but heater should be removed before using the bathroom.
Tub/Shower Does tub/shower have decorative glass doors? Are faucets clearly marked *Hot* and *Cold*? Are shampoos, conditioners, and soaps in pump dispensers? Is there a shower chair available?		Remove glass doors and replace with a shower curtain. Replace or remark *Hot* and *Cold* faucets. Pump dispensers are easier to use than bottles that must be squeezed and/or turned upside down to dispense. Showers can be exhausting. Using a shower chair to rest can help prevent someone from becoming too weak and falling during the shower.
Grab Bars Are there grab bars to make getting into and out of tub or shower easier?		Grab bars should be installed properly and securely into wall studs – not just into tile or fiberglass. Avoid use of suction cups as they can be unreliable.

Home Safety Checklist: Halls and Stairs

Issue	Y/N	Options
Lighting Is lighting adequate?		Use a plug-in night-light. Install light switches on both ends of hallway.
Obstacles Are there obstacles or clutter in hallway?		Remove ALL clutter. Organize and box for proper storage, donation, or disposal—no matter what the item is.
Are there loose floorboards or rugs in hallway?		Repair all loose floorboards. Remove all throw rugs.
Is there furniture in hallway?		Remove all furniture.
Are there doors in hallway?		Keep all doors closed at all times.
Smoke/Carbon Monoxide Detectors Are carbon monoxide and smoke detectors installed?		Install working units on all levels. Replace batteries semiannually.
Handrails Are there handrails in hallway and stairwell?		Install handrails on both sides of hallway and stairwell or secure existing rails.
Stairs Are steps easily seen?		Use neon striping, paint, or duct tape to mark edges of stairs.
Walkers Are walkers easily accessible and transportable?		If possible, keep separate walkers at top and bottom of stairs.

Home Safety Checklist: Kitchen

Issue	Y/N	Options
Lighting Is lighting bright and adequate?		Add task lighting as needed. Bright lights should be located in ceiling above table, countertops, sinks, stove, and in pantry.
Smoke/Carbon Monoxide Detectors Are carbon monoxide and smoke detectors installed?		Install detectors in kitchen. Replace batteries semiannually.
Fire Extinguisher Is there a fire extinguisher in the kitchen?		Make sure fire extinguisher is usable and accessible.
Appliances and their Cords Are there appliances in the kitchen that your loved one cannot or should not use? Are there appliance cords that pose a danger?		Remove appliances that should not or cannot be operated by your loved one on their own. Make sure cords are not near sink or stove.
Counter Clutter Are kitchen counters cluttered?		Keep kitchen counters free of clutter that might cause confusion.
Kitchen Floor Is floor free of tripping hazards?		Remove all rugs, pet food bowls, cords, plants, or any other potential tripping hazards.
Labels Are things visibly and legibly labeled?		Create large-print labels for all switches and containers.

Home Safety Checklist: Kitchen

Issue	Y/N	Options
Cabinets		
Are doorknobs and cabinet handles easy to use?		Label all cabinets and drawers, and replace difficult-to-use handles, pulls, or knobs.
Are the most-used items within easy reach?		Rearrange cabinets if needed to make the most-used items easiest to reach. Get long-handled grabbers if needed.
Is assistance required to open jars and cans?		Find adaptive tools that work best for your loved one.
Stove		
Does it work properly?		Make sure oven door and burner controls are easy to use and work properly.
Is it easy to use?		Label burners and knobs/controls.
		Clear all items on counters near stove.
Should it be used?		If your loved one has a cognitive issue and shows signs of improper stove use, the caregiver must decide to unplug/disconnect the stove.

		Improper use can be things like:
		  placing items on top of burners
		  forgetting something is cooking
		  forgetting that stove or oven is hot

Microwave Oven		
Does your loved one know what it is and how to use it?		Remove or unplug unit if needed.

Home Safety Checklist: Kitchen

Issue	Y/N	Options
Medication Are medications kept in the kitchen?		Designate a cabinet for your loved one's medication. If more than one person in home takes medication, use separate cabinets.
Step Stools Should a step stool be used?		Step stools can be a hazard and must not be used to reach items that are too high. Find an alternative to a stool if items cannot be stored within person's reach.
Refrigerator Is the food inside still good?		Designate someone to throw out old or rotten food. The person you are caring for may not know the difference.
Is the food inside covered and stored properly?		All food in refrigerator and freezer should be tightly covered and stored properly with a label including what it is and date it was stored. Do not store food on top of refrigerator —out of sight, out of mind!
Is a list of emergency contacts readily available on door?		Make sure emergency contact list and information is readily available in "File of Life" pouch on refrigerator door.

Home Safety Checklist: Living Area

Issue	Y/N	Options
Lighting Is lighting adequate?		Room should be evenly lit throughout. Use task lighting and touch lamps as needed.
Flooring and Rugs Is the flooring free of clutter and tripping hazards?		Remove and replace loose floorboards. Area rugs are tripping hazards and should be removed. If floor is carpeted, make sure it has been stretched properly, and ensure there are no lumps or ridges.
Obstacles What are the obstacles in the room? Is there excess furniture? Is there room to navigate? Are there doors in the room?		Remove ALL clutter. Organize and box for proper storage, donation, or disposal—no matter what the item is. Remove unnecessary furniture. Allow 5½ feet in between each piece of furniture to accommodate use of a wheelchair. Keep all doors closed at all times.
Tables Are there glass-topped tables?		Remove all furniture with glass tops.

Home Safety Checklist: Living Area

Issue	Y/N	Options
Tables and Shelving Are tables and shelves full of clutter?		Remove excess clutter from tables and shelves. Organize and box items for proper storage, disposal, or donation.
Chairs and Seating Is the seating comfortable and easy to use?		Use chairs with straight backs, armrests, and firm seats. Make sure seating is a sensible height. Sensible height is if person's thighs are parallel to floor and feet are flat on the floor when seated on the edge of the chair. If needed and possible, add firm cushion to existing pieces to add height. This will make it easier for your loved one to sit down and get up.
Mirrors Does mirror cause fear or confusion?		Mirrors may need to be covered or removed for those with dementia as the person may no longer recognize themselves. Mirrors can be removed or covered with a window shade that can be raised or lowered.
Cords Do they pose a tripping hazard?		Use extension cords sparingly. Secure to baseboards to move them out of the way and prevent tripping.

Home Safety Checklist: Laundry

Issue	Y/N	Options
Lighting Is lighting adequate?		Room should be bright. Add lighting as needed.
Clutter and Organization Is room free of tripping hazards?		If possible, find a place—other than on the floor—to store laundry basket. Remove all unnecessary items and box for proper storage, donation, or disposal.
Supplies Are laundry supplies organized and properly labeled? Can laundry supplies be easily reached without stretching?		Organize and label laundry supplies. Ensure laundry supplies are within easy reach.
Washer and Dryer Are washer and dryer easy and convenient to use? Are dryer lint trap and vent hose cleaned regularly?		Washer and dryer should be located side by side so that wet clothes do not have to be moved from room to room. To prevent fires, clean lint trap and vent hose regularly.
Ventilation Is the room well ventilated?		Keep windows and/or doors open when in room for proper ventilation.

Home Safety Checklist: Basement

Issue	Y/N	Options
Stairs		
Are there handrails on both sides of the steps?		Install railings as needed.
Do railings or steps have loose or uneven wood or potential for splinters?		Repair or replace wood that is loose or splintered.
Are items stacked on the steps?		Remove unnecessary items and box for storage, donation, or disposal.
Lighting		
Is lighting adequate?		Basement should be bright. Add lighting as needed.
Are light switches located at top and bottom of stairs?		Install additional switches as needed.
Clutter and Organization		
Is room free of trip hazards?		Remove unnecessary items and box for storage, donation, or disposal.
		If possible, find a place—other than on the floor—to store laundry basket.
Shelving		
Is shelving sturdy enough to hold items placed on it?		Remove unnecessary items and box for storage, donation, or disposal.
Are items on shelves neatly stacked so they will not fall off?		Shelving should be located at a height that person using it can reach items without stretching.
Frequently Used Items		
Are frequently used items within easy reach?		Organize items so that most-used items are easiest to reach.

Home Safety Checklist: Garage

Issue	Y/N	Options
Stairs		
Are there handrails on both sides of the steps?		Install railings as needed.
Do railings or steps have loose or uneven wood or potential for splinters?		Repair or replace wood that is loose, uneven, or splintered.
Are items stacked on the steps?		Remove unnecessary items and box for storage, donation, or disposal.
Lighting		
Is lighting adequate?		Garage should be bright. Add lighting as needed.
Are light switches located at top and bottom of stairs?		Install additional switches as needed.
Tools and Equipment		
Are sharp tools away from walkways and hung or stored properly?		Hang or store sharp tools properly for safety and to prevent tripping hazards.
Is machinery or equipment blocking walkway?		Remove unnecessary items, and box for storage, donation, or disposal.
Are frequently used tools and equipment easily accessible?		Organize space so that most-used items are easily accessible.
Clutter and Organization		
Is room free of tripping hazards?		Remove unnecessary items and box for storage, donation, or disposal.

Home Safety Checklist: Garage

Issue	Y/N	Options
Frequently Used Items Are frequently used items easily accessible?		If items are used inside the home, consider storing those items inside. Remove unnecessary items, and box for storage, donation, or disposal.
Garage Door Does garage door have an automatic opener?		Automatic garage door openers make it easier to get in and out of the garage. Check batteries in opener and in the main box semiannually.

Home Safety Checklist: Foyer

Issue	Y/N	Options
Lighting Is lighting sufficient inside foyer and outside on porch?		Add lighting as needed.
Doorbell Can doorbell be heard all throughout home?		Repair or replace doorbell so that it can be heard anywhere in the home.
Door, Window, and Peephole Can you see who is standing on the front porch or stoop?		Clear window or install peephole to be able to identify people before opening the door.
Closet Is coat closet easy to use and not too cluttered? Is there room to store hats, scarves, gloves, and boots?		Remove unnecessary items and box for storage, donation, or disposal. If there is no closet, install sturdy hooks for coats, hats, scarves, and gloves.
Doormat Is there a doormat and is it appropriate?		Use an absorbent mat with a non-skid backing. Don't use a dark mat – a darker mat could be mistaken for a hole in the floor.
Door Can door be easily locked? Is there a dead bolt lock on the door?		If a person is in early stages of dementia, doors should be secured to prevent wandering. Install latches high on door so they cannot be easily reached.

Home Safety Checklist: Porch, Yard, Driveway

Issue	Y/N	Options
Lighting		
Do exterior porch and garage lights illuminate entire areas?		Add lighting or replace bulbs with the highest wattage the fixture allows.
Is yard lighting equipped with motion detectors?		If possible, install motion detector lights for safety and security.
Steps and Rails		
Are there sturdy rails to use for climbing up and down stairs?		Repair or replace rails as needed to ensure proper sturdiness and safety.
Are rails smooth and free of splinters?		Repair or replace rails to prevent injury from cracks or splinters.
Are there any loose or wobbly steps?		Repair or replace any loose or wobbly steps to prevent trip/fall hazard.
Are steps slippery in wet conditions?		Add non-slip material to stair treads to prevent them from becoming slippery when wet.
Sidewalks and Driveway		
Do sidewalks and driveway have cracks or loose cement that could be trip hazards?		Repair any cracks or loose cement that could be potential trip hazards. Be aware of tree roots that may affect paved surfaces.
Mailbox		
Is there a clear path to the mailbox?		Make arrangements with the Post Office to have mail delivered to door for a person who is elderly or disabled.

Lighting, Glare, and Color Contrast

Depending on your loved one's visual impairment and individual preferences, you may find it necessary to modify existing lighting, glare, and contrast in the home so your loved one can more easily engage in activities. Here are some tips to help:

Lighting

The following lighting changes could be key in your loved one's safety and ability to perform tasks independently.

- Keep all rooms evenly lit and the lighting level consistent throughout the home, so shadows and dangerous bright spots are eliminated.

- Make sure light switches, pull cords, and lamps are easily accessible for your loved one, particularly if he or she is in a wheelchair.

- Install dark-colored light switch plates on light-colored walls.

- If possible, purchase touch lamps or those that can be turned on or off by sound.

- Be certain that all stairwells are well lit and have handrails.

- Depending on the individual, additional task lighting may be necessary in certain areas of the home.

- Additional lighting for closets and smaller areas may be helpful. Battery-operated push lights are a good option.

<u>Glare</u>

Glare can be caused by sunlight, snow, or light from a lamp. When the light hits a shiny surface, such as a magazine page or even a wall painted with high-gloss paint, the resulting glare can make it difficult for someone with low vision to see.

- Sunglasses can be beneficial both indoors and outdoors for someone who is light sensitive. Offer your loved one the opportunity to try different lens colors to see which works best for them.

- Sunlight can fill the room with light without producing glare. Adjust sunlight coming through windows by using mini blinds and altering their position throughout the day. If mini blinds are not available, use sheer curtains to diffuse the light.

- Be aware when placing mirrors in a room. Mirrors placed across from larger windows can significantly increase the amount of light in a room. This could be beneficial for someone who prefers the additional light.

- Fluorescent lighting can contribute to an increase in glare. Try different types of lightbulbs to see which is most comfortable for your loved one.

- Cover all bare lightbulbs with shades.

- Position chairs and tables so that when your loved one is sitting on a chair or at a table, they are not looking directly at the light coming from a window.

- Cover or remove shiny/reflective surfaces, such as floors and tabletops.

- Use nonskid, nonglare wax to polish floors.

<u>Color Contrasts</u>

Using contrast is a key strategy for people with visual impairments. The more contrast, the easier it is to find and use objects or activity items around the house.

- Put light-colored objects against a dark background.

- Avoid upholstery with patterns for seated activities. Stripes, plaids, and checks can be visually confusing.

- Opt for solid-colored tables and countertops in a neutral tone. Countertops with busy patterns can make it difficult to locate items and can be more difficult to keep clean.

- Contrasting color molding can help improve mobility. When possible, opt for contrast on door and window trim.

- In a room with mostly dark tones, place light-colored pillows or chairs in strategic places to help your loved one find things and get around easily.

- If your loved one must, or is capable of maneuvering stairs, put contrasting stripes on the edges of each stair to make each stair visible and to prevent the stairs from disappearing from view.

Chapter 10

Put Your Mask on First!

There will be many challenges to you personally in this caregiving journey that can and will wear you down. As a caregiver, first and foremost, you must take care of yourself in order to be able to assist your loved one. That might be easier said than done, but please make every effort to do so. The following are some general tips for you, the family caregiver:

About You
- Put yourself first (this is not being selfish)—if you are not in good physical or mental health you cannot help anyone.
- Arrange some time for yourself.
- Keep a strong support system.
- Do not be afraid to ask for help.
- Keep contact with friends.
- Define priorities; do not try to be all things to all people.

Stress

- Recognize your own stress and take steps to minimize. Stress can be exhibited in multiple ways:
    - Anger
    - Helplessness
    - Embarrassment
    - Grief
    - Depression
    - Isolation
    - Physical illness

Burnout

Burnout for caregivers results from physical and emotional exhaustion.

It is important to realize a family member, spouse, or hired caregiver experiences the same emotions as staff in health care facilities, but may not have the needed support system. Suggestions to avoid burnout:

- Know what makes you angry or impatient. Make a list.

- Look for the reason behind behavior.
- Use relaxation techniques, e.g., deep breathing, imagery, and music.
- Ask for help, and accept help when it is offered!

Caregiving is a challenging road with constant twists and turns, from the change in your role/relationship with your loved one, to dealing with the strains of a 24/7 job of caring for that loved one. As much as you may feel like you are alone, please know that you are not. Millions of family caregivers are dealing with the same issues that you are. Do not be embarrassed to share details about what you are experiencing, and do not be afraid to ask for help. There are individuals, organizations, and support groups throughout the country that are available to you. There is also R.O.S.—we were built on the simple mission of our founder's need to help his mother and father during a 25-year battle with Parkinson's and dementia. We understand what you are going through, and we are here to help.

Personal History Form

This is _____'s Personal History

Name: _____

Maiden Name: _____

Preferred Name: _____

Date of Birth: _____

Place of Birth: _____

Name and relationship of people completing this Personal History Form: _____

_____

_____

Diagnosis: _____

_____

Describe the person's personality prior to the onset of the impairment. _____

_____

_____

_____

_____

_____

What makes the person feel valued? Talents, occupation, accomplishments, family, etc. _____
_____
_____
_____

What are the daily living aids that must always be handy?
_____
_____
_____

What are some favorite items they must always have in sight or close by? _____
_____
_____
_____

What is their exact morning routine? _____
_____
_____
_____

What is their exact evening routine? _____
_____
_____
_____

What type of clothing do they prefer? Do they like to choose their own clothes for the day, or do they prefer to have their clothes laid out by someone else?

_____
_____
_____
_____
_____

What is their favorite beverage?

_____

What are their favorite foods?

_____
_____

What will get them motivated? (Church, friends coming over, going out, etc.)

_____
_____
_____
_____
_____
_____
_____

List significant interests in their life, such as hobbies, recreational activities, job related skills/experiences, military experience, etc.

- Age 8 to 20:

  _____
  _____
  _____

- Age 20 to 40:

  _____
  _____
  _____

- Age 40+:

  _____
  _____
  _____

What is their religious background? (Affiliation, prayer time, symbols, traditions, church/synagogue name, etc. Did they lead any services or sing in the choir?)

_____
_____
_____
_____
_____

What type of music do they enjoy listening to, playing, or singing? Do they have any musical talents?

_____

_____

_____

What is their favorite TV program? Movie?

_____

_____

_____

If reading has been a hobby, what authors, topics, or genres do they prefer? Would they listen to audiobooks or books on tape?

_____

_____

_____

_____

Marital status - If married more than once, provide specifics. Include names of spouses, dates of marriage, and other relevant information.

_____

_____

_____

_____

_____

List distinct characteristics about their spouse(s), such as occupations, personality traits, or daily routine.

_____
_____
_____
_____
_____
_____

Do they have children? Be sure to include children both living and deceased. Include names, birth dates, and any other relevant information.

_____
_____
_____
_____
_____
_____

Do they have siblings? Be sure to include siblings both living and deceased. Include names, birth dates, and any other relevant information.

_____
_____
_____
_____
_____

Who do they ask for the most? What is their relationship with this person(s)?

_____

_____

_____

_____

What causes them stress? How is stress exhibited? Are there particular triggers like loud noises or being ignored?

_____

_____

_____

_____

What calms them down when they are stressed or agitated?

_____

_____

_____

_____

How long has it been since symptoms first appeared?

_____

_____

_____

Describe their visual impairment. _____
_____
_____
_____

How long has he/she been visually impaired? _____
_____

Has he/she accepted the visual impairment? _____
_____

What activities do they feel they can no longer participate in as a result of the vision impairment?
_____
_____
_____
_____

List specific activities they enjoyed prior to their vision impairment. _____
_____
_____
_____

Are they participating less with family and friends due to vision loss? _____
_____

What age do you think the person thinks they are?

_____

Do they ask for their spouse but do not recognize them?

_____

Do they ask for their children but do not recognize them?

_____

Do they ask for their mom? _____

Do they perceive themselves as younger? Please describe.

_____

_____

_____

_____

_____

Describe the "home" they remember. _____

_____

_____

_____

_____

_____

Can they tell the difference between someone on TV and a real person?

_____

_____

Other information that would help to bring joy to your loved one.

P = past interest, C = currently engages in this activity, NEW = Has expressed interest in learning				
NAME:				
Interest	N/A	P	C	New
Arts and Crafts				
Knitting				
Sewing				
Crocheting				
Embroidering				
Scrapbooking				
Painting type:				
Coloring				
Woodworking				
Other				
Table Games				
Cards type:				
Bingo				
Dominoes				
Board Games				
Pokeno				
Jigsaw Puzzles				
Other:				
Spiritual				
Attend Church/Synagogue/Temple/Mosque				
Rosary Service				
Bible trivia				
Bible study				
Reading Bible/Torah/Koran/Watchtower				
Other:				

P = past interest, C = currently engages in this activity, NEW = Has expressed interest in learning

NAME:

Interest	N/A	P	C	New
Television / Movies				
Favorite channel:				
Movie types:				
Soap Operas:				
Game Shows:				
Talk Shows:				
Comedies:				
Dramas:				
News:				
Westerns:				
Cartoons:				
Adult Films:				
Other:				
Reading / Writing				
Book Club				
Type of Books:				
Large Print				
Talking Books				
Magazines:				
Legacy Kits/Autobiography				
Newspaper:				
Word Search				
Crossword Puzzles				
Letter Writing				
Other:				

P = past interest, C = currently engages in this activity, NEW = Has expressed interest in learning			
NAME:			
Interest	N/A	P	C	New
Sports Play or Watch				
Exercise:				
Baseball Team:				
Football Team:				
Soccer Team:				
Golf Player:				
Basketball Team:				
NASCAR Driver:				
Tennis Player:				
Other:				
Musical Interests				
Singing				
Listening to Radio/CD Type:				
Live Music				
Play Instrument:				
Movies / Videos				
Outdoor Activities				
Gardening				
Shopping / Outings				
Traveling				
Hunting				
Fishing				
Smoking				
Other:				

P = past interest, C = currently engages in this activity, NEW = Has expressed interest in learning

NAME:				
Interest	N/A	P	C	New
Technology				
Computers / Internet				
Hand-held Video Games:				
TV Video Games:				
Other:				
Volunteering				
Distributing Mail:				
Newsletters:				
Church Groups:				
Service Projects:				
Other:				
Social Activities				
Men's Groups / Ladies' Groups / Young Person's Groups:				
Happy Hour				
Coffee Club				
Intergenerational Visits				
Discussion Groups				
History Groups				
Other				
Cooking:				
Animals:				
Political Interest:				
Manicures				
Other:				

About The Authors and Contributors

Scott Silknitter

Scott Silknitter is the founder of R.O.S. Therapy Systems. He designed and created the R.O.S. Play Therapy™ System, the *How Much Do You Know About* Series of themed activity books, the R.O.S. *BIG Book*, and the R.O.S. Engagement Program used by caregivers around the world.

**Richard Oliver
and the Industries of the Blind**

Richard Oliver lost his vision at the age of 23. He has never let the loss of his vision define who he is or hold him back. Richard is currently the Director of Sales for the Industries of the Blind.

The mission of I.O.B. is to provide opportunities for employment and personal development for people who are blind or visually impaired to achieve greater independence.

Maria Pogorelec, MSN, RN

Maria Pogorelec has over 20 years of nursing experience and earned her BSN from Cleveland State University and her MSN in nursing education from Western Governor's University. Maria's broad nursing experience includes long-term care and skilled nursing, acute care settings, and a medical-surgical unit specializing in the care of adult surgical and orthopedic patients. This experience has given Maria a unique perspective and shaped her outlook to look at the whole person where people need to be treated with dignity and respect and not just the clinical side of care. Whether it is an illness or a decline of physical and mental abilities, these health issues can affect people in many negative ways. Maria has made it a focus to teach caregivers that there is an opportunity to provide support and comfort to a loved one, which can have positive impacts on healing and coping for everyone.

Sheri Shaw
and the Olmsted Center for Sight

Sheri Shaw has been legally blind since birth due to junior macular degeneration. Sheri is currently the Director of Vision Rehabilitation Services at the Olmsted Center for Sight. Since 1907, Olmsted Center has helped adults and children with vision impairments and other challenges live independently without barriers.

Dawn Worsley, ADC/MC/EDU, CDP

Dawn Worsley currently serves as the President of the National Certification Council for Activity Professionals. She is a Certified Activity Director with a specialization in Education and Memory Care, a Certified Eden Alternative Associate, a Certified Dementia Care Practitioner, and an Alzheimer's Dementia Care Trainer. With over 20 years of experience, Dawn is an authorized certification instructor with the National Council of Certified Dementia Practitioners (NCCDP) and a Modular Education Program for Activity Professionals course instructor.

References

1. *The Handbook of Theories on Aging* (Bengtson et al., 2009)
2. *Activity Keeps Me Going, Volume 1* (Peckham et al., 2011)
3. *Essentials for the Activity Professional in Long-Term Care* (Lanza, 1997)
4. *Abnormal Psychology*, Butcher
5. www.dhspecialservices.com
6. National Certification Council for Dementia Practitioners, www.NCCDP.org
7. "Managing Difficult Dementia Behaviors: An A-B-C Approach" By Carrie Steckl
8. Iowa Geriatric Education Center website, Marianne Smith, PhD, ARNP, BC Assistant Professor University of Iowa College of Nursing
9. *Excerpts taken from "Behavior...Whose Problem is it?" Hommel, 2012
10. *Merriam-Webster's Dictionary*
11. "The Latent Kin Matrix" (Riley, 1983)
12. *Care Planning Cookbook* (Nolta et al.2007)
13. "Long-Term Care" (Blasko et al. 2011)
14. "Success Oriented Programs for the Dementia Client" (Worsley et al 2005)
15. Heerema, Esther. "Eight Reasons Why Meaningful Activities Are Important for People with Dementia." www.about.com
16. *Validation: The Feil* Method (Feil, 1992)
17. *Activities 101 for the Family Caregiver* (Appler-Worsley, Bradshaw, Silknitter)
18. Olmsted Center for Sight
19. American Foundation for the Blind
20. Prevent Blindness America. Vision Problems in the U.S.: Prevalence of Adult Vision Impairment and Age-Related Eye Disease in America, update to the 4th ed. Schaumburg, IL: Prevent Blindness America, 2008.
21. "Kaninchen und Ente" ("Rabbit and Duck") from the 23 October 1892 issue of *Fliegende Blätter*
22. www.WebMD.com
23. www.nlm.nih.gov
24. www.nei.nih.gov
25. www.cdc.gov/aging
26. www.alzheimers.org.uk
27. www.caregiver.org

Activities for the Family Caregiver
Series of guides for caregivers by chronic condition

From R.O.S. Therapy Systems
www.ROSTherapySystems.com

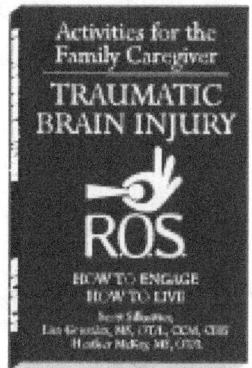

Caregiver Activity Lesson Plans
Series of activity lesson plans with step-by-step instructions

How Much Do You Know About?
Series of themed activity books

For additional assistance, please contact us at:
www.ROSTherapySystems.com
888-352-9788